Josephine Trent-Smith

SIXTY, SAVED, SECURE & SATISFIED

Josephine Trent-Smith

SIXTY, SAVED, SECURE & SATISFIED

Josephine Trent-Smith

EJF PUBLISHING HOUSE
CHICAGO, ILLINOIS

Copyright©2020 by
Josephine Trent-Smith

All rights reserved. No part of this publication may be reproduced, distributed, or transmitted in any form or by any means, including photocopying, recording, or other electronic or mechanical methods, without the prior written permission of the publisher, except in the case of brief quotations embodied in critical reviews and certain other noncommercial uses permitted by copyright law. For permission requests, write to the publisher addressed "Attention: Permissions Coordinator," at the address below. All Bible references are cited from the King James Version unless otherwise noted.

Josephine Trent-Smith/EJF PUBLISHING HOUSE

Publisher's Note: For purposes of confidentiality, sharing names, characters, places, and incidents are a product of the author's imagination. Locales and public names are sometimes used for atmospheric purposes. Any resemblance to actual people, living or dead, or to businesses, ministries, churches, companies, events, institutions, or locales is completely coincidental.

Book Interior Design EJF Publishing House

SIXTY. SAVED, SATISFIED & SECURE!/Josephine Trent-Smith- 2nd ed.
ISBN 978-1-7368985-1-2

.

Dedication

This book is dedicated to my mother and father (now deceased) and to my husband, children, grandchildren, and family.

Special thank you to my niece, Desi who encouraged me to write and publish my first book.

Josephine Trent-Smith

Table of Contents

Introduction..15

This Is Who I AM..17

Girl You're Gaining Weight..19

Sixty-Minutes...25

Saved..31

Secure..37

Satis-fied..41

Bonus

7-Day Journey of Wisdom from Auntie Phine's...45

For Booking Mrs. Smith for speaking engagements contact:

josephinee.smith@gmail.com

Check out her weekly podcast "You Said What" YSW on YouTube.

Josephine Trent-Smith

Introduction

"A little progress each day adds up to big results"
~ Jenn McMahon

It was not until I was leaving my 40's that I finally became comfortable sharing my age with others. Suddenly, I was proud to be going into my 50's, what I called *the 50 cents of my life*. I was excited to look to the future and all that

God still had for me. At the same time, I felt uncertain because I could not find a job. I wondered if working was over for me since I was getting older.

Oh, but God had a plan for me! After turning fifty-five years old, my "double nickel" birthday, I started laughing again as I began to make small investments in myself day by day. I even began taking regular vacations. I looked forward to each day when I could set aside a quiet time to just be with myself. Although I started feeling a little joint pain, I kept it moving. I refused to allow my new digits to stop me from enjoying my life.

Thankfully, I'm not taking any medication currently. I have never had hot flashes although, I do have some kind of rash which flares up every now and again. (LOL!) I embrace my beauty and myself from the inside out and I love that I choose to only wear lipstick.

Chapter 1

THIS IS WHO I AM

"Be the kind of person who makes others want to up their game."
~ Unknown

Letting go of hiding my age was one of the best things I ever did. At fifty, I was half of 100 and it felt good. I was proud to say, "this is who I am and this is how I look!" I used to hide my age because I didn't feel comfortable. I imagined that people were trying to keep track of my age throughout my life. If people did not know me personally, they did not need to know my age. Often, people judge others because of their age. It can become very negative. Comments like, "Girl, you are not so young anymore," are not welcome. That's why I preferred to keep my age to myself. For some reason, some people can't wait to comment on just how old you are. I believe women and men look at age differently. Some men I grew up with saw me as younger, while women I knew were always trying to push my age upward.

It's just me, personally..........

I was feeling good about being healthy and not on any medications when I went for my physical. Some people my age I talked to were having health challenges and needed medications for multiple illnesses. After my physical, I was so happy and thankful when my doctors gave me a good report and told me that I still didn't need to be on any medication. That made me feel so good. Then, I was finally motivated to reveal my age. I wanted people to know that it was possible to live a healthy life and not be on medication. I was very thankful that even in my 50s medications were still not a part of my journey, now if you happen to be a person who has to take medications, do not despair. God always makes a way. Just trust him.

Chapter 2

GIRL YOU'RE GAINING WEIGHT

"Whew, Chile!" When I was approaching fifty, it seemed that no matter what I did, I could not stop gaining weight. Menopause was just around the corner and about to rear its head. But get this, I didn't get hot flashes. I suddenly began itching all over my body.

As for the weight gain, I really could not understand. Although I was eating roughly the same amount, I was still gaining weight. *Oh my goodness*, I wondered, *what in the world is going on?*

What does turning fifty have to do with getting bigger? Do we just accept that it's time to get a bigger size? Older and bigger? I was not feeling good about it at all. It certainly had me feeling a strange kind of way.

Then I started thinking. I will not allow this to make me retreat into the shell I just broke out of. I made the choice that I might as well let that fear go just like I did my worries about age. My new weight and size did not have to take away from my beauty or who I am. *I may be getting bigger, but I am also getting better with who I am.*

I stopped worrying about those people who always had something negative to say about my weight just like they did about my age. Now when they say, "Girl, you're gaining weight!", I don't let it bother me. I know it's true, but I think, SO WHAT? Since I can't hide my weight gain like I could my age, I just embrace it and say, "Yes, I am getting bigger, but I'm looking better!" Once I learned how to embrace my new size, I refused to go back to hiding in my shell.

What Was Different?

I remember turning 47 years old. My monthly "flow" became so heavy. I surely wasn't prepared for that change. It was such an odd time in my life, but I adjusted. Month after month, and year after year, I was pumping myself with pure 100% grape juice to build my energy up. I flowed heavily for eight years straight. Then suddenly it stopped completely when I turned 55. My double-nickel year. It had not been easy, but I got through it!

Leaving my 50's was a breeze. I felt more alive and sexier because I didn't have to be on my period anymore. It was just so freeing for me. I felt at my best. Instead of feeling older, I was feeling younger. I started putting color rinse in my hair and stopped perming it. I was more open to saying what was on my mind, even more than usual. Getting older for me was so liberating.

Josephine Trent-Smith

Since turning 60, I am grateful to God for letting me see a new decade. I have not changed much. I still look the same in the mirror. My body still moves the same. No big changes so far. So, for this, I'm thankful!

I realize that just because my age is getting higher, I can trust God to give me my heart's desire. Now I look forward to my new age every year because I'm going to keep living my best life. If I need to add a little spice, by adding a little hair color, I do it! I will not allow my new age to define how I treat yourself and others. I know that being good to myself and being happy and kind to others is so rewarding, in and of itself. Age brings about a change, but I can choose the change I allow it to bring on and so should you!

Sixty, Saved, Secure, & Satisfied

SIXTY-MINUTES

Josephine Trent-Smith

"Don't put limits on yourself!"

Chapter 3

SIXTY-MINUTES

"Your only limit is you!"
~Unknown

Now, don't get me wrong. I do get ticked off if you come at me wrong. I can tell you off without a cuss word, but for the most part, I believe it's so important to treat others the way you would like to be treated.

As I said goodbye to my 50s (my 50 cents), and approached my 60s (my sixty minutes), I was feeling absolutely wonderful. Jo Baby (that's one of my nicknames) says, "to know me is to love me."

Being sixty is great in so many ways. For one thing, you become eligible for a senior discount. Before you know it, saying your age just begins to flow off your tongue with grace. Sometimes, people would ask me to prove it. I would hear, "Looking at you Auntie Phine, we don't see a senior." Remember, I told you, I don't look 60. I am so thankful for my fountain of youth.

Getting Even Better

When I was fifty-five years old, I decided to make a change in my diet. I gave up eating meat on Labor Day, September 1, 2017.

Making a major change like that after eating meat for over fifty years, required me to take it day by day. I stopped cold turkey. I set my mind to do it and just did it. One day led to another. Month after month, I was meat-free. I was so pleased with myself that every September 1st now, I choose something different to change. I do not let a year go pass without changing something. I don't crave meat, at all. When I go to restaurants, I choose other items on the menu that best fit my new lifestyle.

From time to time, people will ask me what I eat since I cut out meat. "Do you eat protein?" They ask. I let them know I eat avocado, eggs, peanut butter, and beans. But I will not eat meat. Now I do not feel stuffed like I used to feel when I ate meat. After making this lifestyle change, my health improved. I began to lose some pounds. I just feel so much better in my body now. Besides, I feel so much better about myself.

I added something else to make a change. I started small by walking every day. Gradually, I added more steps. I enjoyed it so much that I started jogging in my 60s. I had never done that before and I was so proud of myself. I began by jogging around this huge building where I worked once each day. Then I began to add another lap around the building. Little by little, I added another lap, and another, increasing my distance. I could not believe I was jogging at my age. My healthy future was depending on me.

    I remember when I first decided to start walking, I felt so good. Actually, it felt amazing. Immediately, I saw a difference in myself. You could not tell me that turning 60 could be any better than this. Today I feel so much better in my 60s that I did when I was younger. My confidence soared and I began smiling from the inside out. I thought, *you cannot touch this girl!*

    It is amazing what you can do if you put your mind to it. If you stick to it, you can accomplish goals you might have not thought possible. For me, I discovered that I had to believe it was possible no matter what age I was. These days, my age is not getting in my way. If anything, it is giving me a boost.

"Give yourself permission to change!"

Josephine Trent-Smith

SAVED

Chapter 4

SAVED

"Bless the Lord, O my soul; and all that is within me bless His holy name! Bless the Lord, O my soul, and forget not all His benefits: . . .who redeems your life from destruction.
~Psalms 103:1, 4a

When I open my eyes in the morning, I give God thanks for what He has done for me. Every day is not the same day. I might feel good or maybe a little down but, whatever I am facing, I purpose to go through it with a positive attitude. I try to smile every day. My smile doesn't mean I feel great all the time. It just means I choose to make my day brighter with every smile.

Josephine Trent-Smith

    I discovered that being saved in my fifties was a challenge. I felt called to give up certain things. I was trusting in God to do stuff, that seemed "IMPOSSIBLE" in my eyes. In my mind, things seemed completely out of control and out of my hands. Oh, God had a plan, but I couldn't see it.

I said, "Lord, I know you didn't bring me this far to leave me now." I didn't run and tell anyone about my problems because I knew that people couldn't help me with what I needed. I kept leaning on the Lord to bring me out. Although things were not turning out the way I wanted, that didn't stop me from praying every day. I never missed praying for one day because things were still unsettled around me. I had no money in my bank account, yet God kept filling my spiritual bank account to running over.

I saw God making a way for me out of no way. While I was trying to figure things out, God was already working things out. Things started looking better.

I kept praying. My God! He gave me what He wanted me to have and not what I was trying to get in my own way. He was also clearing up my credit and providing money I didn't have.

I feel like being saved is the only way. It is the only way I know how to live now. Living for Christ has become my life, like breathing air. I love spending time with the Lord. I start my day off with Him because I have so much to say to Him. I can trust Him for He is a place of safety where I share my tears, worries, fears, and concerns. What I give to Him he can take care of. I know my secrets are safe with Him.

The Lord has become my real BFF! I know He loves me; He keeps me all the days of my life. With God, I can always be honest. No matter what is going on, I can tell Him. My BFF, I call Him Father and Savior, He calls me His daughter. I don't just talk the talk; I walk the walk. I don't stray from the course because God has been so good to me.

Josephine Trent-Smith

    Being saved is a blessing. I can't even explain just how good I feel when I talk about the Lord. it's like something inside of me just bubbles up, like a chocolate fountain. Oh, how sweet it is! When I let my guard down and let God take control, that's when I see God bless me. He not only blesses me with material things, but also natural blessings. I am so satisfied being a child of God that I would not go back to doing things my own way for nothing. I wouldn't trade my spiritual heritage for anything in this life. I rejoice that this joy and peace I have walking with the Lord is priceless. He gives "JOY" like a river flowing in me!

*"Friend, **today is a good day to be saved!***"

Josephine Trent-Smith

SECURE

Chapter 5

SECURE

Secure is waking in the morning, showering, putting on body lotion and good smells from head to toe, then adding little enhancements to my eyes and lips, combing my hair, and picking out my outfit for the day. I make sure I don't miss anything by double checking in the mirror. Guess what? I always add a little spice to my day by wearing mix-match earrings. That's just my "Auntie Phine" thing.

I believe when you're in your 60s, you become a new kind of beautiful. You become more secure and confident in your appearance. With a pep in my step, I can strut my stuff. Head held high and no hesitation in my speech, I exude confidence. I feel attractive with every move I make. I move to the beat as to a song playing in my head. I put one foot in front of the other and step into my life.

When I walk to the beat, it may seem as if I'm flaunting, but I'm not. When I get dressed, I choose to change my music to speak to my new day. Being beautiful comes from within and you have to choose to live out your own beauty everyday. At this age, it feels so satisfying to feel good about myself.

Being secure is who I am! It is embracing who I am as a woman. It is taking care of my appearance. I have done this from the time I've known myself. I take time to work on the real me and not care about what other people think of "Auntie Phine." I have become so confident inside and out because what you feel inside shows outside. So, for now having red hair adds a whole new spice to my look. I am proud to be a classy, secure, and mature woman".

Sixty, Saved, Secure, & Satisfied

"At this age, it feels so satisfying to feel good about myself!"

Josephine Trent-Smith

SATISFIED

Chapter 6

SATISFIED

"I am satisfied but I am still learning all aspects and stages of being satisfied."
~Josephine Trent-Smith

I made the decision to be satisfied with my work choice. Even in my 60s, I still work. It's not always easy working in the public, because people are always sizing you up. To be satisfied with my job, I have just decided to let people be themselves. I'll be myself and enjoy what I do on a daily basis. I just keep it moving!

The Menopause

Now this is a whole 'nother something, your body just goes through different changes you cannot always understand or explain. You either have to allow yourself to grow through the process or into the process. But you do have to make a decision how you will deal with it because it comes in different ways for every woman. Become satisfied with who you are, take good care of yourself, look at yourself, and become satisfied with the change because it's only temporary.

Look At Yourself

I am satisfied with the voice the Lord has given me. Whenever I have the opportunity to sing or share a word, I am excited to share the gospel of Jesus Christ with others because it is my saving grace. I believe after you reach a certain age in life, you need to do those things that are best for you! You have to learn to block out all of the background noise! Know who you are because your opinion makes all the difference. Actually, it does not matter what others say but what God says. He has made me a woman of purpose and destiny. I start by looking in the mirror. Look at yourself. Then add or take away whatever you need to, but take time to start listening to your heart, the real you. Begin to reassess who you are and

who you need to be based on what you see. As for me, I see a woman that God is going to take places, so I keep trusting in Him.

Each day is a new beginning. Take a deep breath, smile, and start again. ~Unknown

Josephine Trent-Smith

Auntie Phine's Wisdom

7-DAY JOURNEY OF WISDOM FROM "AUNTIE PHINE"

Wisdom Day One

No matter where you are in life, whether you are married or not, you have to see yourself as an individual. Appreciate the changes that are coming or have come. Your thoughts and feelings are yours. You must choose to not allow the negative stigma of getting older to control your perspective of yourself. Each year of life is a gift. Be okay with who you are evolving into whether you are turning fifty (50 cents) or sixty, because every new birthday is a wonderful gift from God.

Wisdom Day Two

To the next generation growing up, don't let anything hold you back. Don't let your age or what others say stop you from being who you are. Getting older feels so good. Embrace your looks and age. As for me, I am no longer hiding behind my age. These days, I am now moving my age out of the way to live my best life.

Wisdom Day Three

This is for you! If you are on medicine, please take it! That medication is helping you stay alive. There is a saying that when we know better, we do better. Taking your meds is putting your health needs first. Now take that pill, please, for it is keeping you alive and well. You need to be alive to keep moving and doing what you have to do. Be you and be your best! Girl, do not let people judge you and make you feel bad. You can still live your best life.

Wisdom Day Four

No more hiding! You can't spend a full decade hiding because of your weight gain or what people think about you. If you let them tell you how to feel about your weight, by the words they say or the looks they give, you will find yourself living in the prison they've created for you. Weight gain can already have you feeling a certain way. People can see it and it's obvious. But, SO WHAT? I know when you go shopping, you might find yourself liking the dress or outfit in your old size 10. It may be really cute, but instead of stopping there at size 10, you need to move down the rack to your new size. And guess what? Your new size is your Good size! When you put on your new size, own it girl! Look in the mirror and tell yourself "I feel good, and I look good!" It is important to feel good about yourself and how you look. I had to make a decision that I wouldn't allow anybody to body shame me. And that's what I need for you to do. Don't give anyone that power to poke fun at you, box you in, or shackle you with insecurity. Embrace your new beauty.

Wisdom Day Five

Don't put limits on yourself. Don't wait for someone to tell you how good you look. Their opinion should not matter or carry weight unless you allow it to. You have the power to be your own person. Come on, you are your own woman! Always know that your opinion matters. So, begin taking time to do some reflection and get to know yourself. Walk into the new you and find your own new journey. I believe you will find and see that you shine. Now, hold your head up and don't look down. Get your pedicure, get your nails done. Stop dwelling on what others think about you. You don't need their opinions to live. Just LIVE!

Wisdom Day Six

Just look at your own life and see what you need to give up. Maybe it's a habit like smoking or, it may be to stop eating sweets. Whatever it is, make a decision and start today. Take it one day at a time and give yourself the permission to change. You can do it. Whether it takes you 1 month or 6 months, that is up to you. Do whatever works for you, but go as far as you can. If you have to start and stop, start and stop, but do not give up. I believe you will be satisfied with your own choice and surprised by your progress. I can assure you that if you stick with it, you will end up in a better place.

Wisdom Day Seven

Are you saved? What is being saved you ask? Let me tell you why we all need to be saved. We are all God's creation yet we have a broken relationship with Him because of sin. When we are doing our own thing and living to please ourselves with no thought of God, that is sin. We are all born in sin and so we sin. Nothing we do, no matter how good we try to be or what things we do, we can never pay for our sins. Those sins keep us separated from God. But the Bible tells us in John 3:16 that God loves us and that is why he sent his son Jesus Christ into the world. God wanted to reconnect with us! Jesus came to die on the cross to pay the price for our sins and put us back in good standing with God. He came to give us a gift of grace, one we don't deserve and can never pay for. That's why it is called amazing grace! When we pray and accept this gift of forgiveness based on what Jesus did for us, God will forgive us. He will accept us into family and give us a new life, a new purpose, and a new future. Friend, **today is a good day to be saved!** I hope that you will pray to God today and tell him you are sorry for trying to handle life in your own way. Ask him to forgive you and straighten out your life. He wants to fix all the brokenness and make you whole. He is waiting to hear from you.

      Once you are saved, you will begin a new journey of faith in God. Be encouraged because God sees great things in you. Trust in God and then be there for others. Encourage them to also trust in God. Share with them how prayer makes a difference. God can work things out for you. He hasn't given up on you; don't give up on Him. Tell them how being saved has changed your life and how you now live for the Lord.

"Anyone who belongs to Christ becomes a new person. The old life is gone, a new life has begun!"

~ 2 Corinthians 5:17 NLT

www.ingramcontent.com/pod-product-compliance
Lightning Source LLC
Chambersburg PA
CBHW062205100526
44589CB00014B/1956